You Might Be a Boomer If...

Amusing Memories, Timeless Laughs and Classic Quirks from the Good Old Days

Ace Williams
Illustrations Odessa Doolittle

You Might Be a Boomer If...

Amusing Memories, Timeless Laughs and Classic Quirks from the Good Old Days.

Ace Williams
Illustrations by Odessa Doolittle

You Might Be A Boomer If…

1st Edition

Copyright © 2025 by Ace Williams

Illustrations by Odessa Doolittle

All rights reserved including reproductions in whole or in part in any form except by newspaper or magazine reviewers who wish to quote brief passages in connection with a review. No other part of this publication may be reproduced, stored in retrieval system or transmitted in any other form by means electronic, mechanical, photocopying, recording or otherwise without the expressed written permission of the author or Soho Tribe Productions.

Printed in the United States of America.

Dedication

I dedicate this book to my mom who sacrificed so much for our family. If it weren't for her, I wouldn't be here. No matter how tough times were, she always relied on humor and loving support to help get us through.

I want to thank my whole family for the years of fond memories and laughs throughout the decades of the 1960's, 1970's and early 80's. The family reunions, the Fourth of July picnics at the park, visiting grandparents, gathering around the TV, and so many more, those experiences through time accumulated into many of these passages in this book.

You've got one life to live. Try to make it memorable.

Forward

"I am the Unknown Comic, the King of one liners or the Queen of one liners, if I'm wearing chiffon, and though I am sometimes a little backward, I'm writing this forward about the Best Boomers Joke Book I have ever read... or will read, when I learn how to read. And when I do, I will let you know that this is the funniest book you will ever read, except for, perhaps, the "Art of the Deal", by Donald Trump."

The Unknown Comic A.K.A. Murray Langston, comedian, actor, and author of *Journey Thru The Unknown Memoirs of the Unknown Comic*, *The Kardashians Joke Book*, *How to Be Happy (98% of the Time)*, *How to Live Like You're Already In Heaven: An Athiest's Guide To Happiness*, and *The Unknown Comic Scrapbag*.

Contents

DEFINITION	1
GENERATION GAPS	2
TECHNOLOGY	19
HEALTH	25
THEN	36
THEN AND NOW	42
MISCELLANEOUS	58
INDEX	63

DEFINITION

Boomer

boom·er

/ˈbo͞omər/

Noun
INFORMAL

Baby boomers, often shortened to boomers, are the demographic cohort following the Silent Generation and preceding Generation X. The generation is often defined as people born from 1946 to 1964 during the mid-20th century baby boom. The dates, the demographic context, and the cultural identifiers may vary by country.

GENERATION GAPS

You might be a Boomer if… you think Funko Pop is a soft drink that's lost its fizz.

You might be a Boomer if… you think planking is building a wooden deck in your back yard.

You might be a Boomer if... you think a Fidget Spinner is a petite woman with OCD.

You might be a Boomer if... you think a Pokémon Go is a Hawaiian/Jamaican chef with diarrhea.

You might be a Boomer if… you think a Beanie Baby is someone else's ugly kid.

You might be a Boomer if... you think Silly Bandz were The Monkees, Herman's Hermits, and The Archies.

You might be a Boomer if... you think spankz are something you get on your birthday.

You might be a Boomer if… you think a Side Hustle is a dance move.

You might be a Boomer if... when you were first asked to play Cornhole, and you thought it had something to do with a body part.

You might be a Boomer if... when you first heard of Pickleball, and thought it was some kinky thing swingers did.

You might be a Boomer if... you hear about Silicone Bubble Pop and thought it was about a woman's breast implant accident.

You might be a Boomer if... you know what a burn from shag carpet feels like.

You might be a Boomer if... you hear someone ask at your high school reunion, "Where is everybody?

If everyone at your high school reunion is grey haired or bald... you might be a Boomer.

You might be a Boomer if... you think that a BFF is short for Burger and French Fries.

You might be a Boomer if... you used to hang out with friends at your crib, now you're baby-sitting over your grandchild's.

You might be a Boomer if... a jewelry store sales lady says that she wants to show you her bling, and you blush.

You might be a Boomer if… you still wear a mood ring.

You might be a Boomer if… you brag a lot to teens about knowing how to drive a stick shift.

You might be a Boomer if… you still own a stick shift.

You might be a Boomer if… you've ever hitch-hiked across the country.

You might be a Boomer if… you think Coachella is your grand niece's Phys. Ed. Instructor.

You might be a Boomer if… you go to Coachella and you say Woodstock was better.

You Might Be a Boomer if... you've ever seen someone get arrested and you yell out, "Book Em' Dano!"

TECHNOLOGY

You might be a Boomer if... Even though live answering machines are obsolete, when you phone someone, you still keep asking them to pick up.

You might be a Boomer if… you think a terabyte comes from alligators.

You might be a Boomer if… you hear people talking about AI and you ask, "Who's eye?"

You might be a Boomer if... you've ever used foil to get better reception on your TV.

You might be a Boomer if… you've ever asked a stranger where the closest payphone is.

You might be a Boomer if… you think an Earbud is a growth on the side of someone's head.

You might be a Boomer if… you think a flash drive is a naked man in a convertible.

HEALTH

You might be a Boomer if... you get a cramp from a sneeze.

If you sneeze and you pee yourself... you might be Boomer.
If you sneeze and break wind... you definitely are a Boomer.

You might be a Boomer if… you're driving on the road and see a Silver Alert, and notice that the license plate looks suspiciously familiar.

You might be a Boomer if… when you agreed with someone and replied, "Right on". Now, it's what people yell out to you on the road because you left your turn signal blinking.

You might be a Boomer if… when you were young, you could go all night, and now, it takes all night just to go.

You might be a Boomer if… you think that culture wars are about who makes the best brand of yogurt.

You might be a Boomer if… you still feel tired a year after donating blood.

You might be a Boomer if… a concept that blew your mind was "Heavy", now everything FEELS heavy.

You might be a Boomer if… you wear a t-shirt that says, Professional Mall Walker.

You might be a Boomer if… you used to listen to "Stayin' Alive", now, that's your main goal in life.

You might be a Boomer if… you used to say to your girlfriend, "You're outta' sight". Now, it's something you fear your eye doctor will tell you.

You might be a Boomer if... you used to tell people to "Hang Loose", now, it's what most of your body does.

You might be a Boomer if... you remember that Bonanza was both a TV show and a steakhouse.

You might be a Boomer if… you'd greet your friends and they'd give you some "skin". Now, your dermatologist is asking to take samples of yours.

You might be Boomer if… you used to be really funky and groovy. Now, it's what beachgoers say when they see your feet.

You might be a Boomer if... when someone tells you to take a chill pill, and you put your medication in the freezer.

You might be a Boomer if... you still own a bean bag chair, and can't get out of one without help.

THEN

You might be a Boomer if... you've ever sniffed an open bottle of White Out.

If you've ever sniffed paper from a freshly printed mimeograph machine... you might be a Boomer

You might be a Boomer if... you've ever spent ten minutes or more, unraveling the tangled cord of a telephone.

"Hold on, I'll be right back, I'm fixing the phone. " Why does this keep happening all the time?"

You might be a Boomer if... the only phone in your home was connected to a wall on in your kitchen.

If you've ever felt the burn on your index finger from dialing a rotary phone too quickly... you might be a Boomer.

You Might be a Boomer if… you've ever named one of your children after a rock opera.

You might be a Boomer if… you lost your virginity at a drive-in.

You might be a Boomer if… You got lost because you refused to ask for directions, and ignored your wife begging you to look at the road map.

You might be a Boomer if… you've ever done the "shake and blow" to help develop a Polaroid picture.

You might be a Boomer if… you're still waiting for bell bottoms to make a comeback.

THEN AND NOW

You might be a Boomer if… you went to meet your high school sweetheart at the Roller Rink.

You might be a Boomer if… you've ever taken your car to the shop to have them install an 8 track player.

You might be a Boomer if… you've ever saved up your allowance to buy a black light poster.

You might be a boomer if… you've ever said "Ten-four, good buddy" with or without a CB radio.

You might be a Boomer if… you think that a metro-sexual is a creepy dude trying to get freaky on a subway.

You might be a Boomer if... when you were young, you were worried about the draft. Now, you complain about one every time you go to a diner.

You might be a Boomer if... you've had friends from 1969-1973, who suddenly moved to Canada

You might be a Boomer if… you had three channels on your TV when you were a kid. Now, you have over 160, but still watch the same three channels.

If you know first-hand where the phrase "Jumped the Shark" came from… you might be a Boomer.

You might be a Boomer if... you've ever asked a department store clerk, "Where's the tube socks?"

You might be a Boomer if... you used to wear a mini skirt and are appalled to see ladies wearing them now.

You might be a Boomer if… you used to swing in the 60's or 70's. Now, you push your grand kids on one.

You might be a Boomer if… you still have a pet rock, but forgot its name.

You might be a Boomer if… you're upset that no stores sell water beds anymore.

You might be a Boomer if…you let the words "Far Out" slip, and your grand kid points at your belly.

You might be a Boomer if… you used to say "Can you dig it?"
Now, it's what you do in your garden.

If the dispensary sells you better weed than you can grow…
you might be a Boomer.

You might be a Boomer if… you used to be called a stone fox. Now, you have a concrete statue of one in your garden.

You might be a Boomer if… you've told someone back in the day to "Mind your potatoes". Now, it's something YOU do in the garden.

You might be a Boomer if… friends in need would ask you to do them a solid. Now, it's what you hope for every time you go to the bathroom.

You might be a Boomer if... you used to drive a car that was "souped-up". Now, the only thing "souped-up" is your kitchen pantry.

You might be a Boomer if... you used to get "stoked" to go to a party. Now, it's something you do to your fireplace when you're home and cold.

You might be a Boomer if… you remember when McDonald's changed the signs to say over a million served.

You might be a Boomer if... you used to go out to the Disco. Now, when you dance, your disc goes out!

You might be a Boomer if… you used to boogie down. Now, it's what someone says when they see Kleenex stuck to your shoe.

You might be a Boomer if… you thought the movie "Animal House" was a biopic.

You might be a Boomer… if you think that Snoop Dogg is an odd name for Charlie Brown's pet.

MISCELLANEOUS

You might be a Boomer if… you still own a car that doesn't have cup holders, but it does have a cigarette lighter and an ashtray.

You might be a Boomer if… you still like the look of wood paneling.

You might be a Boomer if… you've ever said the phrase, "Pull my finger".

You might be a Boomer if… you regularly enter barbeque contests.

You might be a Boomer if… you own a leisure suit and still wear it.

You might be a Boomer if… you have a bumper sticker on your car that says, "My other vehicle is a golf cart".

INDEX

Broken Down Boomers Comedy Show Social Media links

Website: www.brokendownboomers.com

Facebook   Instagram

Ace Williams Music

Old Folks Home-Song Parody by Ace Williams

Apple Music   Spotify

The Wild Rover (The Lost Version) song by Ace Williams

Apple Music   Boomplay

If you liked this book, leave a review or a rating at your point of sale, such as Amazon. It would mean a lot to me. Thank you.

About The Author

Ace Williams

Flash back, Ace Williams was raised a few years in Ohio and spent most his life in Tampa, to which he calls home. His younger years, he grew up in the late 60's through the 1980's with his 4 siblings and a single mom. Times were not easy, but they were unforgettable.

Flash forward, Ace is now a producer:
(The Broken Down Boomers Comedy Show (TM))
(www.brokendownboomers.com)
Comedian/Producer/Musician/Actor/ & Recording artist,
("Old Folks Home","The Wild Rover (The Lost Version).

Ace has toured with Nat'l. Headliner, Seven Lolli, featured for Kyle Grooms and has performed in clubs across the state of Florida. Ace is a lovable loser who's "Life Ain't Easy" and goes through life being constantly misunderstood.

"From the "Cultural Decade" to the "Me Decade",
I have experienced and observed a lot of these silly snippets of time enclosed on every page. So, kick off your Earth Shoes, settle into your bean bag chair, meditate on life's absurdities from the past to the present and release your inner Boomer.

To book the Broken Down Boomers Comedy Show, contact- info@brokendownboomers.com

The book that abounds with BOOMERISMS
You might be a Boomer if...
You lived thru the 50's 60's and 70's

"This book is a hilarious romp through all things Boomer"-Comedian Richard Weiss, Author of Weiss Cracks

""Ace Williams is the perfect guy to be bringing you a boomer book. He embodies the attitude and easygoing humor that is such a fond feeling of nostalgia whenever I think about about my parent's generation" - Comedian Steven Lolli -Netflix is a Joke Fest., NBC

"Ace is one of the cleverest writers and comedians on the circuit today. His song parodies and turns of phrases will have you bending over laughing. Run don't walk to see him perform. P.S.:Buy his book. Your funny bone will thank you." Comedian/Actor Jay Hewlett, Showtime, Comedy Central

* HEALTH
You might be a Boomer if...
You get a cramp from a sneeze!

* THEN AND NOW
You might be a Boomer if...
If you've ever taken your car to the shop to have them install an 8 track player.

* THEN
You might be a Boomer if...
You lost your virginity at a drive-in

Ace Williams is a lovable loser who's life "Ain't Easy". He understands everyone & is understood by no one. Ace is a comedian, producer, writer and actor & he does song parodies too. He's currently selling out shows with his Broken Down Boomers Comedy Show (TM), booking shows for a national tour.

Soho Tribe Productions
info@brokendownboomers.com

For booking: info@brokendownboomers.com
Visit-www.brokendownboomers.com

The book that abounds with BOOMERISMS
You might be a Boomer if...
You lived thru the 50's 60's and 70's

"This book is a hilarious romp through all things Boomer"-Comedian Richard Weiss, Author of Weiss Cracks

""Ace Williams is the perfect guy to be bringing you a boomer book. He embodies the attitude and easygoing humor that is such a fond feeling of nostalgia whenever I think about about my parent's generation" - Comedian Steven Lolli -Netflix is a Joke Fest., NBC

"Ace is one of the cleverest writers and comedians on the circuit today. His song parodies and turns of phrases will have you bending over laughing. Run don't walk to see him perform. P.S.:Buy his book. Your funny bone will thank you." Comedian/Actor Jay Hewlett, Showtime, Comedy Central

* **HEALTH**
   You might be a Boomer if...
   You get a cramp from a sneeze!

* **THEN AND NOW**
   You might be a Boomer if...
   If you've ever taken your car to the shop to have them install an 8 track player.

* **THEN**
   You might be a Boomer if...
   You lost your virginity at a drive-in

Ace Williams is a lovable loser who's life "Ain't Easy". He understands everyone & is understood by no one. Ace is a comedian, producer, writer and actor & he does song parodies too. He's currently selling out shows with his Broken Down Boomers Comedy Show (TM), booking shows for a national tour.

Soho Tribe Productions
info@brokendownboomers.com

For booking: info@brokendownboomers.com
Visit-www.brokendownboomers.com